ESTHER
Providential Persian Queen

A Bible Study for Women

Lou Ann Mokwa

NORTHWESTERN PUBLISHING HOUSE
Milwaukee, Wisconsin

Cover Illustration: Johnson and Fancher, Inc.
Design: Lynda Williams

All rights reserved. This publication may not be copied, photo-copied, reproduced, translated, or converted to any electronic or machine-readable form in whole or in part, except for brief quotations, without prior written approval from the publisher.

All Scripture quotations, unless otherwise indicated, are taken from the Holy Bible, New International Version®, NIV®. Copyright © 1973, 1978, 1984, 2011 by Biblica, Inc.™ Used by permission of Zondervan. All rights reserved worldwide. www.zondervan.com.

The "NIV" and "New International Version" are trademarks registered in the United States Patent and Trademark Office by Biblica, Inc.™

Northwestern Publishing House
N16W23379 Stone Ridge Dr., Waukesha, WI 53188

www.nph.net

©2022 Northwestern Publishing House
Published 2022
Printed in the United States of America
ISBN 978-0-8100-3187-6
ISBN 978-0-8100-3188-3 (e-book)

22 23 24 25 26 27 28 29 30 31   10 9 8 7 6 5 4 3 2 1

TABLE OF CONTENTS

Dedication

To my dear mother, Eleanor Petersen, who has been the best Christian mother one could ever ask for. Her walk with Christ has been an inspiration to me and is evidenced by her long life of serving others. Her passion for the Word continues into her 96th year, as she is frequently found with her Bible in her lap. Despite her aging mind, she is able to recall and discuss many biblical stories and concepts. I dedicate this study to you, Mom; like Esther, when your time came, you fulfilled your call "for such a time as this." May God give me grace to follow in your path.

"All Scripture is God-breathed
and is useful for teaching,
rebuking, correcting and training
in righteousness,
so that the servant of God
may be thoroughly equipped
for every good work."

2 Timothy 3:16,17

Session 1

INTRODUCTION

Why Esther?

Esther is a true story about a courageous woman who faced insurmountable odds but succeeded in the mission God had placed in her life. But, we say, our lives are littered with strong female characters who succeed, whether they be fictional within our favorite Netflix series and best-selling movies or real-life historical or contemporary figures. Why Esther? Because she was

> unwittingly victimized by an unbearable situation, she stepped up and determined, by God's grace, to make a difference. Throwing protocol to the wind and ignoring all her fears, this woman stood in a gap most of her peers would never have risked. In doing so, she not only exposed and foiled the plans of an evil man, who, like Adolf Hitler, had a violent agenda. She alone saved her nation from extermination.[1]

And most important, her story is given to us as a gift from God in the Bible (2 Timothy 3:16,17). God included this story to teach us to be righteous, to equip us to live in the here and now as godly people, and to trust his sovereign plan—even if that plan involves ungodly people. God commands us in Matthew 4:4, "Man shall not live on bread alone, but on every word that comes from the mouth of God."

There are many good books and studies written about Esther. The few chosen for this study to supplement the Bible will be listed throughout the study and at the end. Pastor Ben Kempfert has reviewed the content for accuracy. I encourage each one of you to study further, using these or any other sources you may find and share them in your group study. Your time will be well spent. I thank you for allowing me to share my research and thoughts with you. Let's begin our journey with prayer:

> *O God, our Maker and Redeemer, we thank you for this time together to learn more about your servant Esther. Let your Word dwell in us, inspire us, and draw us closer to you. In your holy name, we pray. Amen.*

Q 1. **Have you previously been inspired by the story of Esther?**

If so, what about this story inspired you?

SETTING THE STAGE

Where is the book of Esther located in the Bible?

The book of Esther is tucked neatly between the books of Nehemiah and Job in the Old Testament. Nehemiah is sometimes called "Ezra 2" because it is the continuation of the story of Ezra.[2] Despite being located after Ezra and Nehemiah in the Bible, Esther's story actually occurs between the sixth and seventh chapters of Ezra.[3] In the Jewish Bible, it appears in a section called "The Writings." Other books in this section include Song of Songs, Ruth, Lamentations, and Ecclesiastes with Esther at the end.[4] It is also considered one of the historical books of the Old Testament, so we must do our due diligence and review the what, when, and where in the book of Ezra to set the stage for Esther's story.

When and where does our story occur?

The time is roughly 486–465 B.C., and our story occurs after Zerubbabel's rebuilding of the temple but before Ezra and Nehemiah's return to Jerusalem. Briefly, God appointed Zerubbabel as the head of the small tribe of Judah at the time of their return from Babylonian captivity. He was a special servant to God (Haggai 2:23) who reestablished temple worship and led this first band of captives with the high priest Jeshua back to Jerusalem.[5] This is the tiny remnant of Judah Esther will preserve, and this occurs before Ezra and Nehemiah's return with the Jews who had been scattered in Babylon and other parts of the Persian Empire. Esther's story occurs in Susa, the capital of the vast Persian Empire, which we will discuss further in Session 1.

The book of Esther is remembered by the Jews because the annual festival of Purim was instituted, which celebrates the deliverance of this remnant of the Jews during the reign of Xerxes (we will meet him shortly). Without God's divine intervention through the life of Esther, the future existence of the chosen people was at stake and ultimately the appearance of the Messiah.[6] The Bible never ceases to amaze that all roads lead to Jesus.

Who wrote the book of Esther?

There is no definitive answer to this question. Some historians suggest Mordecai, a character who will become very familiar to us and whom we will grow to love. Other sources consider Ezra or Nehemiah to have penned the story, but there is no actual, verifiable proof. It was, however, indisputably a Jew.[7]

There has been considerable debate among theologians, including Martin Luther, whether Esther belongs in the canon of the Old Testament. The word *canon* means "a rod" or a measuring stick with graduated marks to measure length. The canon in reference to the Bible are those books that were judged to be authoritative (God's divine authority) writings. Because neither God nor any worship rituals are mentioned in the entire book of Esther, some argue its divine authority and believe it should not be included in the Old Testament. Additionally, Esther herself does not appear to have been a pious Jew, as there is no mention of prayer, worship rituals including sacrifices, or other forms of Jewish traditions evident in her life. Finally, the book of Esther is not quoted in the New Testament and does not appear in the Dead Sea Scrolls.

Those who deny its inclusion in the Old Testament believe it belongs in the Apocrypha, a collection of books that describe the tumultuous history of the Jews from 200 B.C. to A.D. 100. While we won't have time during this study to sidetrack ourselves with the history of the canon, it is nonetheless interesting and worth mentioning.[8]

Q 2. **Any thoughts on why the important things of God are never mentioned in Esther?**

Those who successfully argued for its inclusion in the canon have "suggested that the book of Esther is a sort of riddle, with God's guiding hand as the unspoken answer. God himself is never mentioned, but his presence and his action are inescapable—especially considering Mordecai's 'for such a time as this' speech in chapter 4. This is even more apparent from our New Testament perspective, where we understand Esther's place in God's salvation history."[9]

Thus, we praise God that the book has survived the arguments of humans, and, in his divine wisdom, he has preserved it in our modern-day Bible to teach us. "The book of Esther has held an important place in the canon because of its strong testimony to God's providence and protection of his people . . . about God's character . . . and sovereignty in a situation that seemed hopeless."[10]

We will use the outline from the People's Bible commentary *Ezra, Nehemiah, Esther* to divide the book into sections for our study.

    I. **The plot against the Jews (1:1–4:17)**

        A. Historical setting (1:1–2:23)

        B. The plot of Haman (3:1–4:17)

    II. **The delivery of the Jews (5:1–10:3)**

        A. Esther's plan (5:1-14)

        B. The rise of Mordecai and downfall of Haman (6:1–7:10)

        C. The triumph of the Jews (8:1–9:32)

        D. The greatness of Mordecai (10:1-3)

HISTORICAL SETTING
(1:1–2:23)

Let's begin by reading all of chapter 1.

King Xerxes I (Greek) is the main character in this chapter. In Hebrew his name is Ahasuerus, but secular history uses the name Xerxes. We will too because it is easier to say and spell. He reigned from 486 to 465 B.C. His father was Darius I, who was king when Zerubbabel rebuilt the temple. Xerxes' reign was followed by Artaxerxes I (Xerxes' son with Vashti), who reigned during the time of Ezra and Nehemiah. The Persian Empire was a vast empire—as indicated in verse 1 and confirmed in historical documents as well. The capital was in Susa, where our story will take place.

It is three years into Xerxes' reign, and an enormous, lengthy banquet is taking place at the start of our story (verse 3) with all sorts of princes, nobles, and military leaders from the empire. This is the first of ten banquets we will observe throughout our study. These celebrations are important as these are where the plots of our story thicken. The purpose of this particular soiree may have been to plan an upcoming war. We see in verse 4 this extravaganza lasted 180 days with a final 7-day banquet at the end. God gives us a glimpse of the beauty of the palace and details of the wine each guest could be served upon request. Historians state that the wine was optional. "It was an incredible display of majesty and power and riches . . . the celebration of a lifetime."[11] Are any of us thinking of what we would wear to all these events?

But wait, there is a guest missing. In verse 9, Queen Vashti, the wife of King Xerxes, enters our story. Little does he know, or maybe he does, but she's having her own feast for the women who aren't at the main banquet. Vashti's party apparel might be even harder for us to figure out!

Q 3. What does King Xerxes command in verses 10-12?

Q 4. And what is Queen Vashti's reply?

King Xerxes' reaction to her refusal gives us an indication of his current state of mind and character. Early in the book of Esther, we find the king to be vainly generous, hot-headed, irrational, temperamental, impetuous, violent, powerful, and wealthy. There are certainly more adjectives we could add, but after six months of non-stop drinking and debauchery, his best character is likely beneath his royal title.

As we read further from verses 13-20, Xerxes calls on his advisors, "men who understood the times." They were court astrologers who pretended to know about the supernatural. Old Testament prophets looked upon them with "derisive scorn" (see Isaiah 44:24,25).[12] In verse 15 he asks them, "What must be done to Queen Vashti?"

Q 5. What is their advice?

So that's the end of Queen Vashti's reign. Or is it? She is deposed, like a modern-day divorce, but not executed, a surprising fact given the king's current frame of mind. Remember, she has a son (actually three sons). Her third son will become king, not during our study of Esther but in the not-too-distant future. In his 18th year, he becomes king, and his mother, "Queen Mother," remains an influence during his reign.[13]

Q 6. From our Christian, biblical perspective, what do we think about the advice given to King Xerxes and the royal edict that "every man should be ruler over his own household" (verse 22)?
As a reference, let us review Titus 2:5; Ephesians 5:22-30; and Galatians 3:28.

Q 7. Have you personally struggled with the verses that command wives to submit to their husbands? How so? If single, have you personally struggled with God's command that men be appointed leaders in not only the home but the church as well?

In Josephus' account, he suggests that "the king was desirous to show her, who exceeded all other women in beauty" wearing only her crown in front of the all-male audience,[14] providing further explanation of her refusal.

Regardless of whether Josephus' suggestion was true or not, God ultimately had the final word. The author of the People's Bible commentary suggests:

> It is unlikely that the writer of Esther intended to use either Xerxes or Vashti as a model of moral virtue. He is simply telling how God prepared the way for Esther to become queen. This chapter reminds us that we should be careful not to conclude that every time the Bible describes people's actions, it prescribes that we should follow their examples. The real lesson in this chapter is not found in the behavior of Xerxes or Vashti but in the power of God, who was invisibly directing human affairs for the ultimate good of his people.[15]

One final note on chapter 1. The history of Xerxes' reign is historically important, as he was planning to wage war on Greece with the "largest army and navy ever assembled." His father had previously waged an unsuccessful attempt on Greece as well. The invasion by Xerxes also failed and is considered "one of the most crucial campaigns in the history of the world" as the Greek victory preserved many of the cultural influences we see in the Western world today.[16]

"Now the king was attracted to Esther . . .
and she won his favor . . .
so he set a royal crown on her head
and made her queen."

Esther 2:17

Session 2

HISTORICAL SETTING

(CONTINUED)

Let us pray:

> Our loving Father, we come before you today to
> thank you for this valuable time in your Word. We
> are excited today to meet and learn more about your
> servant Esther. May her bravery and integrity to
> seek the truth inspire us. Open our hearts and minds
> so we may shape our lives in these truths as well. In
> the name of our loving Savior Jesus, we pray.
> Amen.

Read chapter 2:1-11.

How exciting our journey is about to become! Today we
get to meet Esther! Thankfully the chapter begins after
King Xerxes had cooled his jets. Verse 1 in the New Living
Translation (NLT) states, "King Xerxes' anger had subsided," and the King James Version (KJV) "the wrath of
King Ahasuerus was appeased." He appears to be feeling
a bit of remorse about his decision, as God tells us, "He
remembered Vashti." But at this point, what's done is
done, and God opens the door.

The People's Bible commentary provides some interesting facts from the historian Herodotus about the time
frame and events between chapters 1 and 2. "Four years
have passed between the decree deposing Vashti and the

elevation of Esther."[17] Remember the war being planned at the seven-day banquet in chapter 1? Well, that war occurred during those four years, and King Xerxes' army failed at overcoming Greece. In the historical documents during this time in Greece, the king was accompanied by a wife whose name is Amestris. Most historians agree it was Vashti.

While in Greece, Xerxes, unable to get rid of Vashti, unsuccessfully tried to seduce his brother's wife, so he began an affair with her daughter (yep, his niece), who happened to be married to one of his sons. When Vashti learns of his meanderings, she is none too happy and, in a fit of rage, orders the girl's mother (yep, her sister-in-law) to be mutilated. This sets the course for a possible rebellion against Xerxes. For his own protection, he had to distance himself from Vashti and make good on the original decree to depose her.[18] She is officially divorced and forever gone (from the throne), and as we return to verse 2, a search was made "for beautiful young virgins for the king."

Part of our four-year lapse is the time it took to gather and present these young women to the king. Verse 3 states they came from "every province." Remember, his kingdom was vast, and after they were brought to Susa, they entered the "harem at the citadel of Susa" (let's call it "Spa Susa"), where they received "beauty treatments" before they are presented to the king. This is not just any spa; this is a place where the ladies would spend six months with "sweet odors . . . and with costly ointments" to prepare themselves to meet and entice the king. This is told to us by Josephus, the Jewish historian, who reports that there were "in number about 400" young women brought to the Spa Susa.[19] One in particular was a "damsel in Babylon" who was an orphan being brought up by her cousin Mordecai. Her Hebrew name is Hadassah, or "Myrtle" (verse 7), but her Persian name was Esther, meaning "star."[20]

Thankfully, in verse 7, we meet our Esther. God describes her as having a "lovely figure and was beautiful." In verse 8 she becomes one of the young women subjected to the king's edict and is "taken" (NIV and New King James Version [NKJV]) or "brought" (NLT) to the king's palace. The NIV Study Bible notes state that "neither she nor Mordecai would have had any choice in the matter." Her care is entrusted to the king's eunuch Hegai, and Esther immediately "won his favor" to the point that he provided her with seven maids to attend to her, special beauty treatments, special food, and he settled her into "the best place in the harem" (verse 9).

Q 1. What does the Bible teach us about our new character, Mordecai (verses 5-7,11)?

Q 2. In verse 10, what does Mordecai tell Esther not to do? What would be the reason for this?

Q 3. What compromises would she have had to make to conceal her Jewish heritage and religion?

Q 4. Have you ever been in a situation where you have either formally or informally concealed your Christian heritage/beliefs? How did that situation make you feel? Would you be willing to share this situation with our group?

Let's continue reading verses 12-18.

Verses 12-14 provide information as to the process each girl underwent before her presentation to the king. Verses 15 and 16 give us details about our star's turn to go to the king. GO, ESTHER, GO!

Q 5. What does verse 15 tell us about Esther's character and relationship to Hegai (see verse 9)?

Q 6. What do we see about the providence of God here? (Hint: think Messiah.)

Turn and read Matthew 1:13-16.

Q 7. How do we connect Jesus with this remnant of Jews from which Mordecai and Esther have descended?

Read verses 17 and 18 again.

Oh, happy day! Once the king sets his eyes on our Esther, things move quickly. "He set a royal crown on her head and made her queen instead of Vashti." Josephus tells us, "He married her, and made her his lawful wife." Do we feel another feast coming on? Verse 18 confirms it: "Esther's banquet." (Another outfit. Oh, maybe we can reuse the dress we wore in chapter 1 since it was four years ago.) Josephus documents that he sent "messengers, unto every nation and gave orders that they should keep a feast for his marriage . . . for a whole month."[21] Okay, feasting for a month? One dress is not going to do it!

Let's finish our chapter by reading verses 19-23.

Mordecai "sitting at the king's gate" indicates he had an official position within the Persian Empire. Bible commentaries report that shortly after she became queen, Esther delegated this position to Mordecai.[22]

Q 8. Let's briefly look back to Ruth 4:1. Where did Boaz go when he wanted to discuss business?

23

Back to our current hero Mordecai. If we backtrack to verses 5 and 6, we know he was an exiled Jew from the tribe of Benjamin whose heritage is from King Saul. While at the gate in verse 21, he learns (from another Jew) that two angry *thugs*, Josephus describes them as eunuchs under the employ of the king as well, are plotting an assassination attempt. God tells us that Mordecai reports this information to Queen Esther (we can now officially call her queen), who in turn tells her newly betrothed husband. Xerxes investigates. He wastes no time in deeming them guilty and has them "hanged on a gallows" (verse 23 NKJV).

One other thing to note, verse 20 is a reiteration of what we discussed in verse 10, about Esther concealing her heritage. When God repeats things in his sacred Word, it is of significant importance, and he will reveal that to us soon.

FOR FURTHER STUDY:

- NIV Study Bible notes, Esther 2:3,4. The author is modeling the story of Esther after the story of Joseph in Genesis 41:34-37 and 45:5-7, the Joseph narrative. See Session 4 of our study.

- Eunuchs: a male servant of a royal household in biblical times. These servants were emasculated by castration as a precautionary measure, particularly if they were placed in charge of harems, to prevent an unintended heir to the throne. See Acts 8:26-38 regarding the conversion of a eunuch from Ethiopia under the ministry of Phillip.[23]

- The entry for the name Myrtle in the Bible dictionary states, "The blossom of the Myrtle tree smells better than a rose."

"Because hands were lifted up
against the throne of the LORD,
the LORD will be at war
against the Amalekites
from generation to generation."

Exodus 17:16

Session 3

THE PLOT OF HAMAN
(3:1–4:17)

Let us start with prayer.

> *Dear Lord, you are an awesome God. Thank you for*
> *sharing with us the history of our ancient believers*
> *and the struggles they went through in the cause of*
> *faith. It is truly inspiring and encouraging to us. Let*
> *us bring you glory through the time we share together*
> *in your Word. In the name of our loving Savior Jesus.*
> *Amen.*

Read chapter 3:1-15.

Fast-forward four years in the reign of King Xerxes, who
has our beautiful Queen Esther by his side. In verse 1, a
man named Haman (HAY-man) enters the scene. We are
told he is the son of Hammedatha, who by birth was an
Agagite. We will soon discover what an evil, scheming,
spiteful, manipulative man he is. This tyrant isn't just any
ordinary citizen of the Persian Empire. King Xerxes was
so taken with him that he elevated him to a status that was
"higher than that of all the other nobles." He was essen-
tially prime minister of the Persian Empire.

How does Haman rise to this level in the empire that
the other officials would bend the knee to honor him? He
must have possessed acute political acumen that easily
indoctrinated Xerxes. We are told all the officials bend

the knee, all except Mordecai. It must have been quite the snub, as the other officials noticed it and "day after day" tried to encourage him to reconsider. As you would suspect (and as Mordecai likely knew), Haman became aware of the snub, and in verse 5 we are told, "he was enraged."

Haman's and Mordecai's heritages are of significance. Historians record Haman to be an Amalekite,[24] and it is repeated in verse 10. Why the emphasis on this point that God mentions it twice? Let's take a moment to do a little history lesson on the Jews and Amalekites' ancient past to understand the origin of their respective behaviors.

When the Israelites fled from Egypt, way back in the time of Moses, the Amalekites attacked them. The Amalekites were descended from Esau (the son of Isaac, brother of Jacob).

Read Exodus 17:8-16.

Q 1. In verse 16, how long does it say the Lord will be at war with the Amalekites?

Q 2. And in verse 14, what does God command of the Israelites?

Thus, Mordecai was obedient not to forget, so his intolerant behavior of not paying Haman honor (verse 4) was understandable and admirable but risky given the two drinking buddies he was dealing with.[25] As a Jew, dedication to God was the only authority worthy of reverence, and it created prejudice among the Persians.[26]

Likewise for Haman, his hatred could appear to be driven by the injustice his people suffered at the hands of their god.[27] His anger was directed not only at Mordecai but also at all Jews; it was pervasive and ran deep—he wanted them all destroyed. The price he was willing to pay to the king was high, about half the annual income of the entire Persian Empire at that time.[28] The money was a persuasive technique. He needed to ensure the king could be convinced to issue a decree to destroy them all (verse 9).

Q 3. Given Haman's Amalekite heritage, is his anger justified?

Q 4. Think about a time when you were very angry. Is anger ever justified?

King Xerxes does agree to the plan (verses 10,11), and rather than seeking immediate action against the Jews, Haman determines the date by casting lots or *pur* to decide when to enact the edict. The lot falls 12 months after the edict is written. As a result of Haman's superstition, this gives Mordecai and Esther plenty of time to hatch their redemptive plan.[29] God's plan is so providential, the Jews annually commemorate the date of this decree with the Festival of Purim, the date Esther delivered them from destruction.[30] Part of this celebration includes a dramatic reading of the book of Esther in the synagogue.[31]

Once the king gives his consent, Haman wastes no time in getting the edict written and distributed to the empire (verses 12-14). Josephus records the words of the actual decree in its entirety. This excerpt is quite interesting.

> Whereas I have governed many nations, and obtained the dominions of all the habitable earth, according to my desire, and have not been obliged to do anything that is insolent or cruel to my subjects by such my power, but have showed myself mild and gentle, by taking care of their peace and good order, and have sought how they might enjoy those blessings for all time to come. And whereas I have been kindly informed by Haman, who, on my account of his wisdom and justice, is the first in my esteem, and in dignity, and only second to myself, for his faithfulness and constant goodwill to me, that there is an ill-natured nation intermixed with all mankind, that is averse to our laws, and not subject to kings, and of a different conduct of life from others, that hates monarchy, and of a disposition that is ruinous to our affairs, I give order that all these men, of whom Haman our second father has informed us, be destroyed, with their wives and children, and that none of them be spared, and that none prefer pity to them before obedience to this degree . . . that so when all that have hostility to us are destroyed, and this in one

day, we may be allowed to lead the rest of
our lives in peace hereafter.[32]

Q 5. Any thoughts on the discrepancies in what the
decree is deemed to accomplish and the
descriptions of the men issuing the decree?

Q 6. Back to God's Word in verse 15. After the edict is
issued, what do the king and Haman do?

Q 7. And what was the response of the citizens of Susa?

Praise God this is not the end of our story!

"For if you remain
completely silent at this time,
relief and deliverance will arise
for the Jews from another place,
but you and your father's house will perish.
Yet who knows whether you have come
to the kingdom for such a time as this?"

Esther 4:14 NKJV

Session 4

THE PLOT OF HAMAN
(CONTINUED)
MORDECAI'S RESPONSE

Let us begin with prayer.

> *Dear Lord, we thank and praise you for the gift of your Word. Today, help each one of us see what you intend "for a time such as this" in our lives. We wish to honor you in all we do. Through your grace and mercy, provide in us a willing heart to fulfill your mission. In the ever-loving name of Jesus Christ, we pray. Amen.*

Read chapter 4:1-8.

To refresh our memories, read chapter 3:15. The response of the people of Susa to the edict was bewilderment. The NKJV states they were "perplexed"; the NLT, "the city of Susa fell into confusion." The Persian citizens, excluded in the edict, are stunned. They likely have many friends, neighbors, business partners, etc., who are Jews, and if the edict moves forward, chaos would enter their world as well. Mordecai and the rest of the Jews' response to the edict must have added a dimension of horror at the realization that one day, a year from now, all these people would be exterminated.

Q 1. Read Daniel 9:3 and Joel 2:12-14. Discuss the possible motive of Mordecai (and the rest of the Jews) in the reaction (Esther 4:3) to the edict.

Q 2. What was Esther's response when she was informed about Mordecai's actions (verse 4)?

Esther's "distress" (NIV), "exceedingly grieved" (KJV), clearly tells us she has been secluded from her husband the king, and any news from the "Susa Tribune" has been kept from her as well. However, Mordecai's response alerted her that there was something horrible and significant going on. Likely well known to Esther, the sackcloth and ashes are a Middle Eastern custom representing mourning and a sense of desolation.[33] Esther immediately sends her eunuch Hathak on a fact-finding mission.

Q 3. Where does Hathak find Mordecai (verse 6)?

Q 4. How does Mordecai ensure that Esther gets the facts about what is going to happen (verse 8)? And what is Mordecai's plea?

Remember, up to this point Esther has kept her heritage a secret. Mordecai's request reminds her that the petition is not just for the general Jewish citizenry. These are her people! She is one of them!

Read Esther's response to Mordecai (4:9-17).
Esther's initial response in verse 11 is not one bit surprising or suspect. If she is not summoned to the king, by the king, and she approaches him, the result is death. She verbalizes she hasn't seen her husband in 30 days and finds herself at a vulnerable disadvantage by being unaware of what has transpired. So the fact that she takes the time to calculate her situation and the possible consequences of her actions impresses upon us that she is even-tempered, mature, deliberate, and wise.

Q 5. But are we correct in that assumption, based on Mordecai's response in verses 13 and 14?

Mordecai's "for such a time as this" response to Esther has been heralded as one of the greatest speeches of all time. These words become the climax of the entire book. God has imparted these all-important words not only to Esther but to us as well.

37

ESTHER • PROVIDENTIAL PERSIAN QUEEN

Take a few minutes to reflect on experiences or opportunities in your life that have been your "for such a time as this" moment(s). Share with our group if you are comfortable.

We referred to the Joseph narrative in Session 2. Let's take a few moments to dig a little further into this parallel narrative.

Read Genesis 45:5-7.

In these verses, Joseph is finally revealing himself to his brothers and declaring to them that despite everything they did and all that had happened, it was all God's plan.[34] Please excuse this very simplistic view. We could spend an entire study on this topic (another time?).

Like Joseph, Mordecai exhorts Esther to consider her position given by God and his divine plan for her to redeem his people, if only she will accept this daunting mission. Mordecai knows that there is a possibility Esther may decline her providential opportunity, but he reveals his faith in the one true God by stating in verse 14, "Deliverance for the Jews will arise from another place." His plea, however, is convincing, and we see Esther's faith exhibited in verses 15 and 16. She is acutely aware she cannot do this alone; she needs the support of the Jewish people to achieve her goal.

Q 6. How would Esther's request for the Jews of Susa to not eat or drink for three days support her in her divine mission? (See Ezra 8:21-23.)

Josephus tells us:

> Esther made supplication to God after the manner of her country, by casting herself down upon the earth, and putting on her mourning garments, and bidding farewell to meat and drink, and all delicacies, for three days' time and she entreated God to have mercy upon her, and make her words appear persuasive to the King, and render her countenance more beautiful than it was before, that both by her words and beauty she might succeed, for the averting of the king's anger, in case he were at all irritated against her, and for the consolation of those of her own country, now they were in . . . danger for perishing.[35]

We must remember the power of prayer for our brothers and sisters in their time of need. Casseroles and cakes are fine, but prayer should be considered first.

Q 7. **When discussing the tragedy of a friend or brother/sister in Christ, have you caught yourself saying, "I wish there was more I could do"?**

Our chapter ends with Mordecai's faithful service to our Queen Esther in carrying out all of her instructions. We must consider God's providence, that when Esther became queen, she appointed Mordecai as an official to the king's gate. If he had not been ordained to that position, Mordecai would not have learned of Haman's evil plan.[36]

To prepare for our next section, ladies, gather your ball gowns—we've got a couple banquets to attend!

FOR FURTHER STUDY:

Consider other biblical figures who were in a similar position to Esther's "for such a time as this" and didn't immediately answer or struggled with the call.

- Moses (Exodus 3:7-14)

- Gideon (Judges 6:11-18)

- Jonah (Jonah 1:1-3,17)

- Elijah (1 Kings 19:1-18)

- Jeremiah (Jeremiah 1:1-10)

- Any others?

- Have we considered ourselves in this list?

"When he saw Queen Esther
standing in the court,
he was pleased with her and held out to her
the gold scepter that was in his hand.
So Esther approached and
touched the tip of the scepter."

Esther 5:2

Session 5

THE DELIVERY OF THE JEWS
(5:1–10:3)

ESTHER'S PLAN
(5:1-14)

We begin today's lesson with prayer.

Dear Lord, we come before you today in awe of your mighty power that we will see displayed through your servant Esther. Let us learn from her example on how to rely on you, not only when we have important matters at hand but also every day. Your power is endless and your Word is true, and we thank you for that. In the name of Jesus, we pray. Amen.

Do we remember what we were preparing for at the end of our last chapter? A banquet or two thrown by our soon-to-be heroine Esther!

Read chapter 5:1-8.

It has been three days—another parallel, this time to the narrative of Jesus' death and resurrection. So fascinating! Remember, she has just spent those three days in prayer and fasting, (and Josephus adds) "asking God to have mercy upon her, . . . making her words persuasive . . . her countenance more beautiful."[37] Esther is now in action mode; she has donned her royal robes and approaches the king. In verse 2, we find God has heard her plea. The king "was pleased with her" and offered her the golden scepter to approach him.

Q 1. Let's discuss briefly the range of emotions Esther must have felt. What have the three days in prayer and fasting done to help steel those emotions?

The king is so taken with Esther that in his initial reply he offers her "up to half the kingdom!" Talk about persuasive! We know she had that effect on the king (see chapter 2:17). It boggles the mind that for 30 days he forgot about her. Xerxes' character is described by the historian Herodotus as "an impetuous man, with a roving eye, who was easily swayed by feminine beauty"[38] of which Esther was acutely aware. In God's timing, she uses this to her advantage and has the king's full attention.

Esther's godly character is revealed in her response to the king in verse 4. She doesn't immediately accept his offer of taking half the kingdom, nor is she hasty in answering his question. Instead, she offers to give a banquet—we know he loves a party—to honor Haman, his right-hand man and now her adversary. Does the phrase "keep your friends close, but your enemies closer" ring true here?

Q 2. Leave no doubt, God's plan through Esther is well thought out. She has a banquet ready the same day (verse 4) for Xerxes and Haman. The two waste no

**time in responding to her request (verse 5) and take
full advantage of the opportunity to do what?**

_____(verse 6; fill in the blank).

Xerxes is so pleased, he again asks Esther, "Now, tell me
what you really want," repeating his offer to give her up
to "half the kingdom." She patiently avoids answering his
question and in verse 8 asks Xerxes to come with Haman
to yet another banquet tomorrow; if he is pleased, she will
then ask the king to "grant [her] petition and fulfill [her]
request. . . . Then [she] will answer the king's question."

Q   **3. The People's Bible commentary[39] indicates that
Esther "failed to act decisively . . . when the king
asked her what she wanted." What are our thoughts
on that interpretation?**

The comments in the People's Bible commentary at this
point are similar to the suggested narrative of the historian Josephus, who describes Esther's initial encounter
with the king:

> And thus she came to the king, having a
> blushing redness in her countenance, and
> with a pleasant agreeableness in her behav-
> ior; yet she did go into him with fear; and
> as soon as she was come near to him, as
> he was sitting on his throne, in his royal
> apparel, which was a garment interwoven
> with gold and precious stones, which made
> him seem to her more terrible, especially

when he looked at her something severely, and with a countenance on fire with anger, her joints failed her immediately, out of the dread she was in, and she fell down sideways in a swoon: but the king changed his mind, which happened, as I suppose, by the will of God, and was concerned for his wife, lest her fear should bring some very ill thing upon her, and he leaped from his throne, and took her arm in his arms, and recovered her, by embracing her and speaking comfortably to her and exhorting her to be of good cheer.[40]

Another source states that "from early rabbinic times, Jewish commentators have often thought the idea is to make Ahasuerus (Xerxes) jealous of Haman, i.e., why should the queen be so eager to have him at her party?"[41] That would put Xerxes in the frame of mind that Haman wasn't the man he thought he was.

It is obvious that God has not revealed exactly what was going through Esther's mind and emotions at the time she delayed her request. But God clearly had a plan, a plan that would succeed, and her delay was required for the plan to triumph. God reveals enough for us to know that there is going to be a second banquet.

Q 4. Can we think of any other reasons why Esther may have delayed her response to Xerxes' question?

Q 5. **Have you ever experienced something in your life that was delayed by God's design and, in retrospect, thought, "I am so glad God prevented that plan from succeeding"?**

Read chapter 5:9-14.

When we met and described Haman in chapter 3, we used a few unbecoming adjectives to characterize him. Today, God will reveal that Haman also has an ego as big as the empire and a boiling anger against his foe Mordecai that is bubbling just beneath the surface. In verse 9, his labile emotions are revealed. Initially he is "happy and in high spirits," but by the end of the verse he is "filled with rage against Mordecai." This range of unstable emotions makes him vulnerable to making rash decisions, as we will see in just the next few verses.

He restrains himself for the moment and returns home. Once he gets there, he gathers an audience of his friends and Zeresh, his wife. Once they assemble, his ego goes into high gear. He goes on and on about his wealth and the honor the king has bestowed on him.

He has reason to be proud. The historian Herodotus records that Haman has ten sons. According to Persian culture, this imparts high honor, second only to valor in war. At that time the king would give gifts to large families as "the subject with the most sons."[42] Haman's ten sons will be tragically significant in our study of chapter 9. But today he has another reason to brag. He and he alone (with the king) attended a banquet given by Queen Esther, and yet another invitation was extended to a second banquet tomorrow. Haman is feeling extraordinary and thinks he is at the pinnacle of this game.

47

Q **6. Read Proverbs 11:2 and 16:18. Do these verses hint at what might be about to happen in our plot?**

Haman appears to be in his happy place, doesn't he? But in verse 13 we see his anger regarding Mordecai seep through his Persian pores. The anger must have been so apparent that those around him try to find a solution to reduce his boiling point to a simmer. They want Haman to stay in his happy place, and the only solution they offer is to build gallows (or a pole [NIV]) 75-feet high and have his mortal enemy Mordecai hanged from them. But there is one wrinkle to this plan. . . . Haman needs to convince the king that Mordecai has committed an offense worthy of death. In the meantime, Haman is so confident that the king will agree, he commands the gallows be built. This, however, is a hasty, misguided move.

FOR FURTHER STUDY:

Consider other biblical characters whose ego/greed/anger led them down a path of destruction.

+ Cain (Genesis 4:1-25)

+ Esau (Genesis 25:24-34)

+ Balaam (Numbers 22:5–24:25; Deuteronomy 23:4,5)

+ King Ahab (1 Kings 16:29-34)

+ Absalom (2 Samuel 13:1-25)

+ Add to this list!
(Hint: some of them turned their lives around.)

"So Haman got the robe and the horse.
He robed Mordecai, and led him
on horseback through the city streets,
proclaiming before him,
'This is what is done for the man
the king delights to honor!'"

Esther 6:11

Session 6

THE RISE OF MORDECAI AND THE DOWNFALL OF HAMAN
(6:1–7:10)

We begin today's lesson with prayer.

Dear Lord, bless our study today. We thank and praise you for this time together in your Word. Make our hearts and minds like clay, and mold them as you would see fit to honor and serve you. We look forward to the eternal glory your Son has won for us. Through his saving grace we pray, today and every day. Amen.

Read chapter 6:1-10.

Sleepless nights. We've all had them. Some of us unfortunately suffer from them more frequently than others, and they can be as life-altering as other chronic health conditions. King Xerxes is having one of those nights. Sleep eluded him to the point that he summons his attendants to bring in the "chronicles, the record of his reign, to be . . . read to him." The NIV Study Bible notes state that verse 1 is "the literary center of our account . . . with a series of . . . seemingly trivial coincidences, which bring a critical turn that brings resolution to our story."

Normally, the reading of government records would lull one to sleep, but in this case, the attendants coincidentally read to him the description of Mordecai uncovering the assassination plot to kill the king. Read chapter 2:23. How could the king have forgotten a thwarted assassination attempt? Only God knows, and in his timing, the significance of this past event is revealed to the king in the middle of the night.

The king is so moved by Mordecai's act of bravery and shocked by the fact that "nothing has been done for him" that he immediately summons whoever is in the court. Another seemingly trivial coincidence, Haman just happens to be in the court. Was he having a sleepless night as well, pacing the floors, practicing his speech to convince the king about hanging Mordecai on the gallows? Again, these details aren't provided, but who better than Haman, his prime minister, his best friend and closest ally, to consult on proffering a plan for "the man the king delights to honor"? Unfortunately for Haman, his super-inflated ego prevents him from thinking beyond himself, and in verses 7-9, he reveals what he hopes to be a self-aggrandizing view of how such a man should be esteemed.

Haman can already feel the royal robe adorned upon his shoulders and see the magnificent royal horse he will ride, adorned with a royal crest on its head. King Xerxes is impressed and wholeheartedly approves of the plan. And in verse 10 he tells Haman what to immediately do, with the caveat that the plan is not for him but for Mordecai the Jew.

Q 1. Not that we wish Haman any ill will (God will judge him), but what words or phrases in verse 10 may have struck Haman the deepest? Can we hear Proverbs 11:2 ringing in our ears?

Read verses 11-14.

Imagine for a moment being on the streets, witnessing Haman leading Mordecai in a procession and proclaiming, "This is what is done for the man the king delights to honor!" While we aren't given those details, we can suppose Haman's appearance must have been demonstratively deflated after the blow he's suffered. Baldwin, a biblical commentator, shares a fascinating view: "The words Haman had to proclaim must have been as gravel in his mouth."[43]

Q 2. In verse 12, where does Mordecai return after the procession? What does this say about his character?

Q 3. Have you ever thought you deserved a higher station in life than what God has provided?

The opposing behaviors of Mordecai and Haman after the procession has ended further illuminate the nature of their respective temperaments. Instead of letting this high honor that was bestowed on him go to his head, we are told Mordecai returns to his usual routine at the king's gate. God provides us with an example of godly character. Haman, however, "rushed home, with his head covered in grief" and shares the gloom of his situation with his wife and friends. They do not offer him a lot of hope. They know he has cooked his goose. Before they can offer any solace or sound advice (not like they've done that before), he is summoned to the banquet Queen Esther has planned. We're not invited to this party, but God will allow us to be flies on the wall . . .

Read chapter 7:1-10.

It is now the second day, the second banquet. Queen Esther is in the driver's seat (or saddle). Upon arriving at the dinner, Xerxes and Haman assume their normal routine (verse 2) and begin drinking wine. It doesn't take long, however, for the king to address the queen, repeating the question he asked her in chapter 5:3. Clearly, the king had one objective at this dinner, and he wasted no time getting to the point. This night was for the queen, not reveling with Haman.

Verses 3 and 4 reveal Queen Esther's humble plea. Her approach in answering the question must have been foreign to King Xerxes. Remember, he was normally surrounded by the bold, rash, and vainglorious requests of Haman and others when approached. But here is this beautiful woman with a simple petition to save herself and her people from slaughter and annihilation.

Q 4. **What effect do we think the second half of verse 4 had on her request?**

Master negotiators would likely tell you her request should have been broader, more comprehensive and inclusive in getting more than what she was really asking for.

After all, he was offering her half the kingdom. But God in his infinite wisdom uses her humble request to shock the king to his core. And in verse 5 we find it succeeds in doing just that.

King Xerxes is stunned beyond belief and demands, "Who was the author of this misery?"[44] Esther now boldly reveals the truth of the contemptible man whom God just happens to place at the scene. Most translations of this verse use the same three words to describe Haman: "adversary, enemy, and wicked." The king takes one look at Haman and knows what she is saying is true, and the anger that resides in the king's heart is ignited. Uncharacteristically, he decides to take a moment to compose himself by going out into the palace garden.

Q 5. Our scheming adversary knows his life is on the line. What final mistake does Haman make in verses 7 and 8?

Based on the king's response after he returns, his attendants waste no time covering Haman's face, signaling his doom. The eunuch Harbona informs the king what building project Haman recently engineered to hang Mordecai upon. Without much hesitation the king commands, "Impale [Haman] on it!" The chapter ends with God telling us, "The king's fury subsided."

Josephus records:

> And from this I cannot forbear to admire God, and to learn thus his wisdom and his justice, not only in punishing the wickedness

55

of Haman, but in so disposing it, that he should undergo the very same punishment which he had contrived for another; as also because thereby he teaches others this lesson, that what mischiefs anyone prepares against another, he, without knowing of it, first contrives it against himself.[45]

Esther has not yet fulfilled her commission. In the next chapter, she continues in her endeavor to ensure her people are no longer in danger.

FOR FURTHER STUDY:

- God names the eunuch Harbona in verse 9. Does his name ring a bell (see chapter 1:10), and what impact might he have on our story?

- Consider Haman's fate and the law of Moses in Deuteronomy 5:20 and 19:16-21, which states that someone who falsely accuses another should befall the same fate he planned for the accused.

- Esther's wise appeal to the king is reminiscent of the appeal Abigail made to David when he was preparing to kill her evil husband Nabal in 1 Samuel 25:4-35.

"In every province and in every city
to which the edict of the king came,
there was joy and gladness among the Jews,
with feasting and celebrating.
And many people of other nationalities
became Jews because fear of the Jews
had seized them."

Esther 8:17

Session 7

THE TRIUMPH OF THE JEWS
(8:1–9:32)

Opening prayer:

> *Dearest Lord Jesus, we are in awe of you and what you teach us through your Word. We know your judgment can be harsh and swift, and as sinners we deserve nothing less. But your grace and forgiveness are so sweet. Thank you for saving us from the Hamans that live within each of us. Remind us of your blessings through this time in your Word. In the name of our loving Savior. Amen.*

Read chapter 8:1-10.

God's Word is so amazing. Our story could have ended with the hanging of evil Haman, but Esther knows God's work is not finished and does not relish in the victory just won, despite "that same day" King Xerxes gives her the entire estate of Haman. This isn't just any estate; it was extensive (as we learned in chapter 5). And remember, there are ten sons! Talk about a power grab! But Esther is not swayed by the immense endowment achieved by the victory. Instead, she remains vigilant to her mission.

Her people are not yet safe; the edict calling for the death of the Jews remains. With her loving cousin Mordecai now in the king's presence, wearing none other than the signet ring taken off the hand of Haman, she pleads with the king. She remains so distraught, she is "falling at his feet and weeping" (she "besought him with tears" [verse 3 KJV]). Xerxes is so taken by her emotion that he once again extends the gold scepter to Esther, who must now compose herself to explain the source of her agony.

Q 1. Verses 3 and 5 both repeat something we learned about Haman's heritage in chapter 3. Why do you think God emphasizes this again?

Reading verse 5, God reveals to us a shining example of humility in Esther's request to the king. The effect of her servility on King Xerxes is revealed by his immediate call to "write another decree . . . at once" (verses 8,9) to replace the original edict. Royal decrees in Persia could not be revoked. They needed to be replaced by a new decree.[46] The NIV Study Bible notes comment on the "literary symmetry" achieved in these verses when compared to chapter 3, as they are almost identical, regarding the writing and publication of the decree to all the people. The new edict written for the Jews was very similar to the edict written against them, a complete reversal of fortune for the Jewish people and championed by our Queen Esther.

Read verses 11-17.
The date of the new edict is noted in verse 12 and is "two months and ten days after the proclamation of Haman's edict."[47] This date allowed the Jewish people "eight months of preparation for any attack."[48]

Verse 15 reveals the rise to prominence of our hero Mordecai within the king's empire. Some commentators state he is now the prime minister of Susa.[49] He rides out into the city of Susa, among his people, in radiant royal garments, sharing in the "joyous celebration" when the "edict of the king came" (verses 16,17). The KJV in verse 17 states, "The Jews had joy and gladness, a feast and a good day."

Q 2. **What does the end of our chapter tell us about the non-Jewish citizens of Susa?**

The NLT states, "And many of the people of the land *became* Jews themselves, for they feared what the Jews might do to them" (emphasis added). The People's Bible commentary states, "Many people allied themselves with the Jews in order to share in their triumph."[50] This is the only place in the Old Testament the word *became* is used. Its Hebrew meaning is "conversion (to Judaism)."[51]

Q 3. **Can you think of a New Testament example of a similar day when Jews and non-Jews were converted to Christianity?**

Q 4. Consider how your character reflects and influences others. Can we apply the example of Mordecai and his influence on the Persians to ourselves?

Read chapter 9:1-6.

The day of reckoning for the Jews has arrived. The enemies of the Jews put up some sort of struggle, but with God on the side of the Jews, their opponents are overpowered and defeated. Even the government officials helped the Jews. That's how influential Mordecai had become.

Q 5. What does the end of verse 3 tell us about why the government officials (likely non-Jews) helped them? How do we think Mordecai, in his new, powerful position, influenced them to the point of fear seizing them?

Five hundred enemies of the Jews perished that day.

Read verses 7-19.

These verses tie up the loose ends of Haman's family, and we see Queen Esther remains in the favor of the king. He continues to grant her wish, not only in the Jews being granted an additional day to blot out their enemies but also in dealing with the all-important sons of Haman. Verse 7 tells us that they have already perished at the hands of the

Jews, but Queen Esther wants their bodies displayed by impaling them on poles (verse 13).

This would appear to be out of character for our sweet, humble Esther to ask for such a gruesome exhibition in the city square. But God states three times, "They did not lay their hands on the plunder" (verses 10,15,16). Remember, the non-Jewish citizens of Susa had been living under the impression from the original edict seen in chapter 3:8. There is a certain people whose customs are different, who do not obey the king's laws. The citizens of Susa should not tolerate them. Thus, they need to be annihilated. These feelings may not have easily dissipated with a new edict. Esther needed to protect the Jews against the persistent enemy, and God was providing an opportunity "for such a time as this" to do so. She was honoring God and preserving his people by completely eliminating the foe once and for all. Verse 16 tells us that 75,000 perished in the two days at the hands of the Jews.

Q 6. What did they do on the third day (verse 18)?
   What parallel do we see here?

The People's Bible commentary states: "The real purpose of the scriptural account is not to defend or excuse the action of the Jews. Rather, it is to show how God acted in history to preserve his chosen people, so that the promise of the Messiah could be fulfilled."[52]

Read verses 20-32.

Here we read the details of the Festival of Purim. The name of the festival comes from the word *pur*, which refers to lots Haman had cast in his plan to destroy the entire Jewish population. This is a major two-day holiday for the Jews and appears alongside the other major festivals of Passover, Pentecost, and Tabernacles instituted by Moses at God's command. The events to commemorate this festival may have been written by Mordecai to help remind the Jews of God's faithfulness, given their history of short memories.[53]

It is celebrated in February and is like a combination of New Year's and Halloween, with costumes worn by children and merrymaking. They read the entire book of Esther publicly and sing festive songs. Interestingly, whenever Haman's name is mentioned during the reading, they interrupt the reading with noisemakers and singing.[54] Even in death, poor Haman cannot find peace.

Q 7. **What are some other interesting points about these verses that strike us?**

FOR FURTHER STUDY:

• For comparison, consider what the Philistines did when they found Saul and the bodies of his fallen sons among the dead (1 Samuel 31:8-10) and Esther's request to display Haman's sons after their deaths (Esther 9:13).

• Consider David's promise to Jonathan and how he fulfilled his promise by restoring the land that belonged to Saul and taking in Mephibosheth (Jonathan's son) to always eat at his table (2 Samuel 9).

THE GREATNESS OF MORDECAI
(10:1-3)

Read chapter 10:1-3.

God's postscript to the book of Esther honors none other than our hero Mordecai.[55] In it, God comments that this history is also recorded in the historical books of Media and Persia. Remember, this was a vast empire where Gentiles were the majority of the population and they ruled as such. This tiny remnant of the Jews was preserved and elevated by God through his servants Esther and Mordecai in becoming queen and second-in-command of the empire, respectively. Given our current world in all its trials and tumults, let us use this story to remind us that God is and always will be in control.[56]

Let us close with the hymn verse from "What God Ordains Is Always Good."

What God ordains is always good;
His will is just and holy.
As he directs my life for me,
I follow meek and lowly.
My God indeed
In ev'ry need
Knows well how he will shield me;
To him, then, I will yield me.

Christian Worship: Hymnal, 844

FOR FURTHER STUDY

- Chapter 8:11-14: There is some controversy about whether the Jews were being unethical in regard to their enemies in response to the new decree. Some opine that the Jews were given permission to slaughter even the wives and children of any people who would attack them. Another view is that the Jewish people may not have carried out what was permitted but killed only the men who attacked them (see chapter 9:6). Another possibility is that the edict refers to the women and children of the Jews, i.e., the assault mentioned was expected to be directed against the men, women, children, and possessions of the Jews for which they then could arm themselves.[57]

- Ethically consider some of the choices/behaviors Esther made in achieving her mission: Did she take advantage of Xerxes' flaws? The killing of Haman's sons? Did the end justify the means? How does this lead us to act?

- Festival of Purim. Read about the other major festivals instituted by Moses in Leviticus 23:5-8; Numbers 28:26; Leviticus 23:34-44.

- Mordecai is now second-in-command, which recalls Joseph's ascendancy in Egypt. See Genesis 41:37-45.[58]

Answer Key

1. Have you previously been inspired by the story of Esther?

It has intrigued me as it is only one of two books of the Bible named after a woman. The book also reveals God's complete sovereignty and power over our lives and circumstances, which ultimately strengthen our faith.[59]

If so, what about this story inspired you?

Other than the above, the more I researched the story, the more intriguing it became. Looking at each character and his or her respective personalities—responses to controversy and chaos—led me to reflect and self-examine who I am as a Christian. While not always comfortable, God's Word is "alive and active. Sharper than any double-edged sword, it penetrates even to dividing soul and spirit, joints and marrow; it judges the thoughts and attitudes of the heart" (Hebrews 4:12).

SETTING THE STAGE

2. Any thoughts on why the important things of God are never mentioned in Esther?

It has been noted to be a "literary device to heighten the fact that it is God who controls and directs all the seemingly insignificant coincidences" (of which we will see many throughout our study). Further, "God's sovereign rule is assumed at every point ... and is made all the more effective by the total absence of reference to him." [60]

HISTORICAL SETTING

3. What does King Xerxes command in verses 10-12?

He commanded his seven eunuchs who served him to bring before him Queen Vashti, wearing her crown (some have suggested only her crown before the all-male audience), in order to display her beauty to the people and nobles.

4. And what is Queen Vashti's reply?

In verse 12 we are told that when King Xerxes' message was delivered to the queen, she refused to come.

5. What is their advice?

Because she refused to appear when commanded by the king, she not only offended the king but "all the nobles and the peoples" of the king's empire (verse 16). They felt her refusal would become an example for other women to defy their husbands and rise up against them. It is interesting to think these advisors were so afraid of the women in their lives and the chaos that would ensue, exemplified by their disrespect and discord, that they created a law "which cannot be repealed" (verse 19) commanding women respect their husbands.

6. From our Christian, biblical perspective, what do we think about the advice given to King Xerxes and the royal edict "that every man should be ruler over his own household" (verse 22)?
As a reference, let us review Titus 2:5;
Ephesians 5:22-30; and Galatians 3:28.

Galatians 3:28 reminds us that our relationship with God is determined solely through faith in Christ. It is not dependent on our gender, race, marital or social status, etc. Ephesians 5:22-30 outlines God's will for Christian husbands and wives in their relationships with each other, motivated by Christ's saving love for us. Titus 2:5 expands briefly on the God-pleasing character of a Christian woman in marriage. By contrast, King Xerxes and his advisors, as well as Queen Vashti, were pagans who knew nothing of the love of Christ or God's plan for marriage. As pagans, their motivations and behavior were guided not by the Word of God but by their own self-interests and self-preservation. Ultimately, "the real lesson in this chapter is not found in the behavior of Xerxes or Vashti but in the power of God, who was invisibly directing human affairs for the ultimate good of his people."[61]

7. **Have you personally struggled with the verses that command wives to submit to their husbands? How so? If single, have you personally struggled with God's command that men be appointed leaders in not only the home but the church as well?**

   Answers will vary. Allow plenty of time for discussion as this is a difficult concept.

   These are not easy concepts, and they become particularly difficult if the husband is not a believer or men who are in authority in the church do not follow the intent of God's plan. This plan was established in Genesis when God created man. Paul explains this in 1 Timothy 2:13,14, "For Adam was formed first, then Eve. And Adam was not the one deceived; it was the woman who was deceived and became a sinner." But what if the man or husband does not fulfill his God-given authority? God raises up the woman to influence the man "when he sees the purity and reverence of [the woman's life]" (1 Peter 3:2).

ESTHER • PROVIDENTIAL PERSIAN QUEEN

SESSION 2 HISTORICAL SETTING (CONTINUED)

1. What does the Bible teach us about our new character, Mordecai (verses 5-7,11)?

He was a Jew from the tribe of Benjamin. Briefly, this is the tribe that descended from Benjamin, the youngest son of Jacob. The royal city of Jerusalem lay within the boundaries of the tribe's territory.[62] Israel's first king was Saul (a Benjaminite). Saul's family were the Kish and Shimeites who had been carried into captivity 120 years earlier. These people were Mordecai's immediate ancestors.[63] He was likely an accountant and employed by the king as a government official.

He was very committed to his family, shown by his adoption of Esther, a cousin who became an orphan. His fatherly love of Esther was apparent as he daily "walked back and forth" in the courtyard near where the harem was kept (verse 11).

2. In verse 10, what does Mordecai tell Esther not to do? What would be the reason for this?

He forbids her to reveal her nationality and family background. God does not reveal why Mordecai instructed her to do this, but God's timing is perfect: she will reveal this information to the king at the proper time.

3. What compromises would she have had to make to conceal her Jewish heritage and religion?

She would have had to abandon her worship rituals, including praying, fasting, dietary laws, and dress. More important, she would have had to adopt the Persian harem customs to ensure her heritage remained concealed until such time as God guided her to reveal it.

4. **Have you ever been in a situation where you have either formally or informally concealed your Christian heritage/beliefs? How did that situation make you feel? Would you be willing to share this situation with our group?**

One of the many blessings about living in our country is the freedom we have in practicing our religion. Currently, there are no legal penalties for practicing Christianity. We must thank God for giving us that freedom each and every day. However, many in our society laugh and mock some of the things we believe, considering them old-fashioned and archaic. It is in those situations where sometimes it is easier to keep quiet than to defend our beliefs. That is exactly what Satan wants us to believe. In each circumstance, we should ask for the Holy Spirit to guide our actions and responses. Or, share the situation with a trusted Christian friend and discuss ways in which we can better share our beliefs in truth and love.

5. **What does verse 15 tell us about Esther's character and relationship to Hegai (see verse 9)?**

Think back to our passages on submission. Esther submits herself (likely humbly) to Hegai and "asked for nothing" other than what he suggested. It appears their relationship was mutually respectful, and, as we see in verse 9, he took special care of her.

6. **What do we see about the providence of God here? (Hint: think Messiah.)**

Without her Christlike submission to God's plan, the Jews would have been exterminated and with them the ancestral line to Jesus. Our God is an awesome God!

7. **How do we connect Jesus with this remnant of Jews from which Mordecai and Esther have descended?**

Through Jacob.

8. **Let's briefly look back to Ruth 4:1. Where did Boaz go when he wanted to discuss business?**

"Meanwhile Boaz went up to the town gate and sat down there." The gate was the town hall of ancient Israel, the normal place for business and legal transactions. [64]

SESSION 3   THE PLOT OF HAMAN

1. **In verse 16, how long does it say the Lord will be at war with the Amalekites?**

"From generation to generation." Since Moses wrote these words, it has been roughly 950 years, or 25 generations. [65]

2. **And in verse 14, what does God command of the Israelites?**

To "write this on a scroll as something to be remembered."

3. **Given Haman's Amalekite heritage, is his anger justified?**

The Amalekites are an ancient, wandering tribe descended from Esau's grandson Amalek. They appear in the Bible in the time of Abraham and wandered the land settled by the Israelites, frequently attacking them and thus becoming bitter foes. The fighting lasted for generations, from Gideon, King Saul, and David. Ultimately, they were defeated by the Simeonites and remained dispersed at the time of our story. [66]

The anger in Haman's heart would appear to be out of proportion, given how long it has been since the Amalekites' ultimate defeat. But bitterness and rage toward others not of our own heritage has been a sin since the fall of Adam and Eve and is not unique to us today. Thus, we need to identify it as such, repent, and ask God to open our hearts toward those who are not of our own race or ethnicity.

4. **Think about a time when you were very angry. Is anger ever justified?**

James 1:19,20: "Everyone should be quick to listen, slow to speak and slow to become angry, because human anger does not produce the righteousness God desires." But we do see examples of righteous anger throughout the Bible. In John chapter 2, when Jesus cleared the temple, he was provoked by a righteous anger that the temple was being turned into a business. This righteous anger is anger directed at sin, which causes man to violate God's law; this anger is not violent, abusive, excessive, or out of control. It is an anger that comes from a love for the sinner to turn away from sin and seek the righteousness of God. "Whoever dwells in the shelter of the Most High will rest in the shadow of the Almighty" (Psalm 91:1). When we continue to dwell in God's shadow, "we have nothing to fear . . . and we will escape God's righteous anger." [67]

5. **Any thoughts on the discrepancies in what the decree is deemed to accomplish and the descriptions of the men issuing the decree?**

The statement "showed myself mild and gentle, by taking care of their peace and good order, and have sought how they might enjoy those blessings for all time to come" is out of character for the king and particularly Haman, who we can be assured knew and had a hand in formulating the edict. This verbiage is a ruse to the Persian people to get them to abide by the decree.

The next statement: "Kindly informed by Haman, who, on my account of his wisdom and justice, is the first in my esteem, and in dignity, and only second to myself, for his faithfulness and constant goodwill to me." We will learn how full of himself Haman is as our story progresses, but at this point the king is totally taken into the deception weaved by our antagonist.

6. **Back to God's Word in verse 15. After the edict is issued, what do the king and Haman do?**

   They sit down to drink. The Hebrew translation for "to drink" is "drink, wet one's whistle, booze, imbibe." It literally means to have a spicy or alcoholic beverage.[68]

7. **And what was the response of the citizens of Susa?**

   They were bewildered.

SESSION 4   THE PLOT OF HAMAN (CONTINUED)/ MORDECAI'S RESPONSE

1. **Read Daniel 9:3 and Joel 2:12-14. Discuss the possible motive of Mordecai (and the rest of the Jews) in the reaction (Esther 4:3) to the edict.**

   The response is one of repentance. The act of tearing one's clothes and putting on sackcloth and ashes was a call to repentance. But God does not want an outward display of penitence unless there is a change of heart and true repentance.[69]

2. **What was Esther's response when she was informed about Mordecai's actions (verse 4)?**

   She was distressed and sent him clothing to replace the sackcloth.

3. **Where does Hathak find Mordecai (verse 6)?**

   In the square in front of the palace gate.

4. **How does Mordecai ensure that Esther gets the facts about what is going to happen (verse 8)? And what is Mordecai's plea?**

   He sent an actual copy of the decree with Hathak for Esther to read for herself. Thus there would be no miscommunication or interpretation of what the edict stated. Mordecai asked Hathak to explain the decree and urged her to go to the king to beg for mercy and plead for her people.

5. **But are we correct in that assumption, based on Mordecai's response in verses 13 and 14?**

Most Bible commentaries and study notes do not agree that Esther was taking time to calculate her situation and the possible consequences of her actions, impressing upon us that she is even-tempered, mature, deliberate, and wise. The People's Bible commentary is of the opinion that her delay was due to fear that she would be in mortal danger by approaching the king.[70] This fear was predicated on the fact that she had not seen the king in more than 30 days and had possibly fallen out of favor (forgotten or replaced) as queen.[71] Whatever the reason, God used this delay to teach us an important lesson on how to approach difficult tasks and situations.

6. **How would Esther's request for the Jews of Susa to not eat or drink for three days support her in her divine mission? (See Ezra 8:21-23.)**

This period of fasting and praying imparted humility before God, asking for deliverance for herself and, in turn, the Jewish people when she approached the king.

7. **When discussing the tragedy of a friend or brother/sister in Christ, have you caught yourself saying, "I wish there was more I could do"?**

Yes, personal tragedy in our own and others' lives makes all of us feel helpless. Prayer should be considered one of the highest priorities during these tragic, painful times, but not only then. Prayer should be part of our daily routine. When I consider that I can have God's attention any day, any time, I feel so foolish at how often I fail to be with him in prayer. Consider the following passages for encouragement:

Ephesians 6:18: "Pray in the Spirit on all occasions with all kinds of prayers and requests. With this in mind, be alert and always keep on praying for all the Lord's people."

1 Peter 3:12: "The eyes of the Lord are on the righteous and his ears are attentive to their prayer."

SESSION 5   THE DELIVERY OF THE JEWS/ ESTHER'S PLAN

1. **Let's discuss briefly the range of emotions Esther must have felt. What have the three days in prayer and fasting done to help steel those emotions?**

   We see in chapter 4:16 that Esther is determined to do what she must, despite the risk of death. This determination was evident before she spends three days in prayer and fasting. This time of seclusion provided her the time to focus on God, his will, and the duty she had to her people. It anchored her to God's faithfulness, which she learned because she was raised in Mordecai's house.

2. **(Fill in the blank)** *Drink.*

3. **The People's Bible commentary indicates that Esther "failed to act decisively . . . when the king asked her what she wanted." What are our thoughts on that interpretation?**

   Simply, the delay was providential. God used Esther's indecision for his plan to succeed.

4. **Can we think of any other reasons why Esther may have delayed her response to Xerxes' question?**

   Answers will vary.
   We will see as we study further the time between chapters 5:9 and 7:1, the verses become a rich tapestry with God's developing plan. Oh, God's Word is so amazing!

5. **Have you ever experienced something in your life that was delayed by God's design and, in retrospect, thought, "I am so glad God prevented that plan from succeeding"?**

   There are many examples in life of God delaying plans for something to unfold, something that is so much better or at a better time in your life.

Consider David's prayer to God to allow him to build a permanent temple (2 Samuel 7:27). But God did not grant David's request; instead, he imparted this blessing to his son Solomon (see 1 Kings 5:1–6:38). Franzmann comments, "God denied David the lesser blessing of building the temple but the infinitely higher blessing was the spiritual temple, that God would grant when he spoke to Mary in Luke 1:32,33."[72] "He will be great and will be called the Son of the Most High. The Lord God will give him the throne of his father David, and he will reign over Jacob's descendants forever; his kingdom will never end."

6. **Read Proverbs 11:2 and 16:18. Do these verses hint at what might be about to happen in our plot?**

   Proverbs 11:2: "When pride comes, then comes disgrace, but with humility comes wisdom." "The Hebrew word for pride comes from a root that means to 'boil up,' a reference to raging arrogance or insolence."[73] It is so appropriate as we've already learned Haman's pride is fueled with vain self-glorification and humility is not in his DNA.

   Proverbs 16:18: "Pride goes before destruction, a haughty spirit before a fall." Unfortunately, Haman is blinded by his pride; and while the glaring warning signs are everywhere, he is oblivious.

SESSION 6   THE RISE OF MORDECAI AND
the Downfall of Haman

1. **Not that we wish Haman any ill will (God will judge him), but what words or phrases in verse 10 may have struck Haman the deepest? Can we hear Proverbs 11:2 ringing in our ears?**

The king instructs Haman to "do just as you have said," not for you, Haman, but for Mordecai the Jew, and "leave out nothing you have suggested" (NLT). The fire of hatred that so burned in Haman's heart against Mordecai was doused and extinguished. "Pride goes before destruction" (Proverbs 16:18). Let Haman's fall serve as a warning to all of us.

2. **In verse 12, where does Mordecai return after the procession? What does this say about his character?**

Mordecai returns to the king's gate. He has no presumptions of the new favor he has found within the kingdom; he remains dutiful and steadfast to where God has placed him, and he humbly returns there to continue his work.

3. **Have you ever thought you deserved a higher station in life than what God has provided?**

Consider Ephesians 4:16: "From him [Christ] the whole body, joined and held together by every supporting ligament, grows and builds itself up in love, as each part does its work."

"While every part of the body has a different role, every role is important! We tend to downplay our gifts and abilities. Maybe we like to think that we're the appendix in the body of Christ and serve no purpose, but God makes every part of the body important."[74]

Mordecai provides us with an exemplary model of being not only content but humbly committed to the station God provided in his life. There's nothing wrong with prayerfully seeking a new and improved station in life by pursuing education, finding a more suitable job, or adapting to life's changes. But we must always focus on doing it to the best of our abilities in service to God and the church.

4. What effect do we think the second half of verse 4 had on her request?

The depth of her humility is evident here. If death, destruction, and complete annihilation of her people were not the directive of the edict, it would not be worth bothering the king. Her people have been through generations of suffering, including slavery, but she cannot stand by when the Jewish people are at risk of being snuffed out of history forever.

5. Our scheming adversary knows his life is on the line. What final mistake does Haman make in verses 7 and 8?

Haman is desperate to preserve his life, and thus he pleads for Esther to intervene on his behalf. However, the way he approaches her is once again misguided. "Haman drapes [himself] over the couch in a compromising position . . . grasping . . . with a desire to implore her favor." Once the king comes in after composing himself in the palace garden, he is stunned! Would Haman really consider "ravaging" the queen? This was against the strict rules the Persians had about anyone other than the king approaching his harem.[75]

FOR FURTHER STUDY:

6. God names the eunuch Harbona in verse 9. Does his name ring a bell (see chapter 1:10), and what impact might he have on our story?

He may have been one of the seven advisers who appear in Ezra 7:14, indicating he may have had some knowledge of the "Law of your God," which were the five books of the Pentateuch, written by Moses.[76] Harbona was comfortable enough in his role as adviser that he did not hesitate to speak the truth to the king he served.

SESSION 7   THE TRIUMPH OF THE JEWS/
THE GREATNESS OF MORDECAI

1. **Verses 3 and 5 both repeat something we learned about Haman's heritage in chapter 3. Why do you think God emphasizes this again?**

   The "long-standing enmity between the Jews and Amalekites" ultimately could have culminated in thwarting God's redemptive plan for mankind.[77] Thus, the importance of repeating this should not be lost on the reader.

2. **What does the end of our chapter tell us about the non-Jewish citizens of Susa?**

   They likely observed the veracity of the celebrations of the Jews and were so influenced (and fearful of their non-Jewish heritage) that they became Jews.

3. **Can you think of a New Testament example of a similar day when Jews and non-Jews were converted to Christianity?**

   The day would be Pentecost. Read Acts 2:1-5,11. The verses following that passage are what the non-Jews witness and hear from Peter as he recounts the Old Testament prophet Joel's words: "In the last days, God says, I will pour out my Spirit on all people" (Acts 2:17). This information changes their hearts, and they ask Peter and the apostles, "Brothers, what shall we do?" (Acts 2:37). Peter tells them, "Repent and be baptized, every one of you, in the name of Jesus Christ for the forgiveness of your sins. And you will receive the gift of the Holy Spirit" (Acts 2:38). "About three thousand were added to their number that day" (Acts 2:41).

4. **Consider how your character reflects and influences others. Can we apply the example of Mordecai and his influence on the Persians to ourselves?**

   People will notice our character if we exhibit fruits of the Spirit every day. Paul tells us in Galatians 5:22,23, "The fruit

*of the Spirit is love, joy, peace, forbearance, kindness, good-
ness, faithfulness, gentleness and self-control." We can all
influence others when we display these characteristics.*

5. **What does the end of verse 3 tell us about why the
government officials (likely non-Jews) helped them?
How do we think Mordecai, in his new, powerful
position, influenced them to the point of fear
seizing them?**

   *They were afraid of Mordecai. How Mordecai influenced
   them to the point of fear likely has to do with his strength of
   character, integrity, and, most important, his faith and fear
   of the one true God. His faith was shining brilliantly for all
   to see and influenced many souls to repent and follow God.*

6. **What did they do on the third day (verse 18)?
What parallel do we see here?**

   *They celebrated with feasting and joy. The Jews were rejoicing
   and praising God for his faithfulness, which preserved them
   from death. Comparatively, on Easter we celebrate the empty
   tomb, praising God for his Son Jesus who overcame death for
   us forever. Matthew 28:5,6, the basis of our Christian faith!*

7. **What are some other interesting points about these
verses that strike us?**

   *These verses are a synopsis of the book of Esther. It is a
   resplendent story within the macrocosm of our ever-faithful,
   loving, eternal God and his plan to redeem all humankind.
   He will not fail, good will triumph over evil, love will ban-
   ish hatred and sickness, and sadness will be no more. (See
   Revelation 7:15-17.) This is the joy for which we live and
   should celebrate every day!*

FOR FURTHER STUDY:

8. Ethically consider some of the choices/behaviors Esther made in achieving her mission: Did she take advantage of Xerxes' flaws? The killing of Haman's sons? Did the end justify the means? How does this lead us to act?

As we previously read in the discussion of chapter 5, Esther was aware that the king was easily swayed by feminine beauty. God, in his wisdom, made her beautiful and she did not waste this asset but utilized it to God's glory. We are all members of the body of Christ and have been given different talents, and "God has placed the parts in the body, every one of them, just as he wanted them to be" (1 Corinthians 12:18).

She was also wise in using the king's predilection for being wined and dined to create a pleasing atmosphere in which to execute her plan. It was a way to entice Haman as well to be present at the scene when the truth emerged.

The killing of Haman's sons, while gruesome and not something to be taken lightly, was again part of God's plan. As humans, we sometimes need reminding that God must be revered and feared (Proverbs 1:7; Isaiah 11:2,3). This fear and reverence help develop a Christian character of obedience (Romans 6:23). Unfortunately, not all will enter the glory God has prepared for us (Matthew 7:21). God will judge us all (Hebrews 10:30,31).

Only God can answer if the end justified the means. But as Christians, we must take heed, examine ourselves as we read these biblical stories, and praise God for his gift of grace (Ephesians 2:8,9) through our Lord and Savior, Jesus Christ.

Leader's Guide

SESSION 1   INTRODUCTION/HISTORICAL SETTING

Welcome and thank all the participants for coming to the first session of *Esther: Providential Persian Queen.* Especially welcome those who are new to the group, and make them feel comfortable. Consider having everyone introduce themselves, and possibly ask them to answer the first question from the introduction on page 8: "Have you previously been inspired by the story of Esther?" Make this voluntary. Those who are new to Bible study may feel intimidated by this. But it will help to create dialogue.

Review a few housekeeping items such as the location of the Bible study, review the timetable for the sessions, and if a larger and more formal class, provide a written schedule of when and where you will be meeting. Direct everyone to the location of the bathrooms, parking, entrance to the facility, etc. Collect a list of participants with names, phone numbers, and e-mail addresses so you can update everyone on class date changes, cancellations, etc. Make sure you are prompt about starting on time and finishing within the allotted time. Being reliable will prevent people from being distracted or discouraged from studying God's Word.

Do an overview of the book. Direct them to the table of contents as well as the endnotes (references) and answer key. Encourage participants to use the answer key only as a supplement to their own answers. Encourage each of them to take the time to marinate in this story and reflect personally on what God through his Word is teaching each participant on an individual level as each studies it. Offer the opportunity for questions throughout the first session to encourage open discussion throughout the entire study.

You may structure your study in a couple of ways: *(a)* have the participants review a specific section of the study and Bible readings before class and spend your time together discussing the content and study questions, or *(b)* read the book and Bible readings in class (this will take more time) and review the study questions briefly in class. As the facilitator, choose a structure, but if you find your participants aren't likely to complete the work prior to class, reviewing it in class is fine—just allow for the extra time. As well, there are a few review questions provided in the Leader's Guide to refresh people's memories before starting new each session and new content; use these as you like. How quickly you proceed through the material is completely up to you and your group. A rough estimate is seven to eight hour-long sessions.

Since most students haven't prepared ahead of time for the first session, begin by joining together in prayer. One is provided on page 8, or you can use your own personalized prayer. Then ask for volunteers to read the introduction, historical setting, and accompanying Bible reading (Esther chapter 1) out loud. Rotate readers. Review the questions. This will give you an idea of those participants who are familiar with the story and those who are completely new to it. Take mental notes for those you can rely on if you get stumped by a question.

One very important thing I have learned is you do not need to have the answers for every question the group poses. Like me, many of you may not have had formal Bible training, so tell the group you will query your pastor and provide them with the information the next time you meet. Or, get participants to do a little research of their own and come back with the answers. It is a great way to create enthusiasm for your study.

There are a few sessions that have "for further study" at the end. These are completely optional and are for those students who want to delve deeper. Some bullet points are just interesting factoids I discovered.

Close each session with the date and time for your next session and what you will be studying. Prepare to close each session with prayer (or you can assign this task). Don't stress about creating your own prayer; consider using the Lord's Prayer, a prayer from the hymnal, a hymn verse (spoken together), or prayers found online at wels.net.

Finally, spend time in prayer yourself before facilitating, asking God to give you wisdom and strength.

SESSION 2   HISTORICAL SETTING (CONTINUED)

Welcome the group back to our study. Review any questions students may have. Clear up any housekeeping items. Begin with prayer.

Before we start chapter 2, let's review some of the important events and people we learned about in chapter 1.

1. **Who were the main characters we met in chapter 1?**

   King Xerxes, Queen Vashti, seven eunuchs, experts (or court astrologers).

2. **What was happening as we start our story?**

   A large banquet that lasted 180 days.

3. **What did we say was the purpose for such a long, protracted banquet?**
   To plan a war.

4. **Who was missing at the banquet?**
   Queen Vashti.

5. **What did Queen Vashti do when she was summoned by the king?**
   She refused to come.

6. **What were some of the reasons she may have refused to come (according to the historian Josephus)?**
   He requested she come wearing only her crown in front of an all-male audience.

Turn to page 13 in your booklets as well as Esther chapter 1. Ask a volunteer to read verses 19-22.

7. **In reply to her refusal, what did the experts advise the king to do?**
   See verses 19 and 20. "Issue a royal decree . . . that Vashti is never again to enter the presence of King Xerxes. Also let the king give her royal position to someone else who is better than she." And this decree would state that every man be ruler over his household (verse 22).

8. **The end of verse 19 is the window God is providing for our story to unfold. What does this passage say?**
   "Let the king give her royal position to someone else who is better than she."

Read chapter 2:1-11.

After reading these verses, pose the following questions (not in the study part of the book):

9. **How many years have passed between the decree deposing Vashti and the elevation of Esther?**

   Four.

10. **What three things occurred during that time?**

    A war in which Xerxes was defeated by the Greeks, the official divorce of Queen Vashti (wasn't that ugly?), and gathering the young ladies and bringing them to Spa Susa.

Review the six questions on pages 16, 17.

11. **What did Mordecai do for the king?**

    Uncovered a plot to assassinate him.

12. **And where did this get recorded?**
    (Hint: see verse 23.)

    In the book of the annals in the presence of the king. Please remember this detail, it will become very important later in our study.

The session will continue until the end of Esther chapter 2. Follow the book (read book sections out loud if needed) and discuss questions.

To prepare for the next class, the group should read all of Session 3.

Close with prayer.

SESSION 3   THE PLOT OF HAMAN

Welcome the group back to our study. Review any questions students may have. Clear up any housekeeping items. Begin with prayer.

Let's begin with a brief review of Session 2.

Review with these questions (not in the study part of the book):

1. **How many years was it between Queen Vashti saying no to the king requesting she appear at the banquet to Esther being presented to the king?**

   Four years.

2. **And what three things occurred in the span of those four years?**

   A war in which Xerxes was defeated by the Greeks, the official divorce of Queen Vashti (wasn't that ugly?), and gathering the young ladies and bringing them to Spa Susa.

3. **How did God describe our Esther? What were her other names?**

   "Lovely figure" and "beautiful." Hadassah and Myrtle.

4. **What is the name of Esther's elder cousin who raised her? And what do we know about his heritage?**

   Mordecai. He was a Jew from the tribe of Benjamin. Briefly, this is the tribe that descended from Benjamin, the youngest son of Jacob. The royal city of Jerusalem lay within the boundaries of the tribe's territory. Israel's first king was Saul (a Benjaminite). Saul's family were the Kish and Shimeites who had been carried into captivity 120 years earlier. These people were Mordecai's immediate ancestors. He was likely an accountant and employed by the king as a government official. He was very committed to his family, shown by his adoption of Esther, a cousin who became an orphan. His fatherly love of Esther was apparent as he daily "walked back and forth" in the courtyard near where the harem was kept.

5. **While at the city gate, what did Mordecai discover and report to the new Queen Esther?**

   He uncovered the plot being hatched by Bigthana and Teresh to assassinate the king and told Esther, who in turn told her newly betrothed husband Xerxes (2:21).

6. **What happened to Bigthana and Teresh when the king found out?**

   They were immediately hanged on the gallows (verse 23). This is an important point to remember, as we will discover in chapter 6!

7. **And where did this get recorded? (Hint: see verse 23.)**

   In the book of the annals in the presence of the king. Please remember this detail; it will become very important in Session 6 of our study.

Read chapter 3:1-15.

8. **Moving on to Esther chapter 3: Who enters our story? And who was he?**

   Haman, an Amalekite. He was the king's "prime minister" and very powerful (see verse 1).

9. **What did the king require all the royal officials to do to honor Haman (verse 2)?**

   Kneel.

10. **Who refused to kneel and honor him? And what was Haman's seething reaction to this refusal?**

    "Mordecai would not kneel down or pay him honor" (verse 2). In verse 6, Haman looked for a way to destroy all the Jews.

Read Exodus 17:8-16.

Review and discuss the seven questions in the book.

To prepare for the next class, the group should read all of Session 4.

Close with prayer.

SESSION 4   THE PLOT OF HAMAN (CONTINUED)/ MORDECAI'S RESPONSE

Welcome the group back to our study. Review any questions students may have. Clear up any housekeeping items. Begin with prayer.

Have a volunteer read the assigned verses.

After reading the first eight verses, review with these questions (not in the study part of the book):

1. **In chapter 4:1, what did Mordecai do in response to Haman's edict to annihilate the Jews?**
   "He tore his clothes, put on sackcloth and ashes, and went out into the city, wailing loudly and bitterly."

2. **What was the motive behind these actions?**
   It was a call to repentance.

3. **In addition to this outward display, what is the most important part of true repentance for Mordecai and us?**
   A change of heart.

After chapter 4:8-17 is read, review with these questions (not in the study part of the book):

4. **What was Esther's immediate response when she learned about the edict? (See verses 10,11.)**
   She was fearful because she had not seen the king in more than 30 days, and approaching the king without being summoned could have resulted in immediate death.

5. **What was Mordecai's response to Esther?**
   (Hint: the climax of the book!)

   *"Do not think that because you are in the king's house
   you alone of all the Jews will escape. For if you remain
   silent at this time, relief and deliverance for the Jews
   will arise from another place, but you and your father's
   family will perish. And who knows but that you have
   come to your royal position for such a time as this?"*

Reread verses 15-17 and review these questions (not in the
study part of the book):

6. **What is Esther's plan in response to Mordecai's
   "for such a time as this" speech?**

   *To pray and fast for three days and nights and afterward
   approach the king.*

To prepare for the next class, the group should read all of
Session 5.

Close with prayer.

SESSION 5   THE DELIVERY OF THE JEWS/ ESTHER'S PLAN

Welcome the group back to our study. Review any questions students may have. Clear up any housekeeping items. Begin with prayer.

1. **We had a brief discussion about God not mentioning prayer while Esther was fasting (4:16). It was noted in the People's Bible commentary that praying was implied. It was also mentioned that similar to God never being mentioned in the entire book of Esther, his providence in this story is the elephant in the room.**

   Regarding the implication of prayer along with fasting, the NIV Study Bible notes state, "The omission of any reference to prayer or to God is consistent with the author's intention; absence of any distinctively religious concepts or vocabulary is a rhetorical device used to heighten the fact that it is indeed God who has been active the whole narrative."

2. **Why did we think Esther delayed her response to King Xerxes' question in chapter 5:3,6?**

   Again, referring to the NIV Study Bible notes, "The author uses these delays as plot retardation devices that sustain the tension and permit the introduction of new material on Haman's self-aggrandizement" (verses 11,12). God painted a picture of Haman, so there was no question about his intent and character.

To prepare for the next class, the group should read all of Session 6.

Close with prayer.

SESSION 6   THE RISE OF MORDECAI
AND THE DOWNFALL OF HAMAN

Welcome the group back to our study. Review any questions students may have. Clear up any housekeeping items. Begin with prayer.

1. **In chapter 6, what did the king request when he had a sleepless night (see verse 1-3)?**

   He ordered the book of the chronicles be read to him.

   And what did he discover (verse 3)?

   Nothing had been done to recognize Mordecai, who prevented the assassination attempt.

2. **What did the king do immediately?**

   He asked Haman in verse 6, "What should be done for the man the king delights to honor?"

Think of all the trivial coincidences in these few verses: the king's inability to sleep, his requesting reading of the annals, the reading of the passage reporting Mordecai's past kindness, Haman's building of the gallows, Haman being conveniently located in the court when the king requested, and Haman developing a self-aggrandizing plan to honor what he thought would be for him. From the NIV Study Bible: "All these events testify to the sovereignty of God over the events of the narrative. Incidental events that occurred earlier, now take on crucial significance."

3. **In chapter 6:12, where does Mordecai return after the procession that honored him?**

   Mordecai returns to the king's gate. He has no presumptions of the new favor he has found within the kingdom; he remains dutiful and steadfast to where God has placed him, and he humbly returns there to continue his work—a lesson we should all apply through self-examination.

To prepare for the next class, the group should read all of Session 7.

Close with prayer.

SESSION 7   THE TRIUMPH OF THE JEWS/ THE GREATNESS OF MORDECAI

Welcome the group back to our study. Review any questions students may have. Clear up any housekeeping items. Begin with prayer.

Last time we read chapters 6 and 7. Today, we are going complete our study reading chapters 8, 9, and 10. We will find our story ending on a very, very happy note! After all the deceit we have witnessed by the sinister prime minister of Susa, Haman, we are now going to revel in the glory that the truth can bring once it is revealed. Briefly, let us set the stage to where we are going to start today.

At the second banquet given by Queen Esther for King Xerxes and Haman, she finally answers the question the king has been so anxious to know the answer to. Let us read this question in chapter 7:2. She reveals to Xerxes exactly what has been happening, and in verse 6 the king becomes aware that Haman has not been what Xerxes thought but is, in fact, a vile enemy to the Jews.

1. **How does the king respond? (Hint: see verse 7.)**
   The king went out into the palace garden in a fit of rage.

2. **What does the king decide about Haman's fate after he returns from simmering his anger in the garden? (Hint: see verse 10.)**
   Haman is executed ("impaled" in NIV, "hanged" in NKJV).

Let's move on to chapter 8:1-10.

I hope you have enjoyed this study of Esther. If you have any questions or wish to talk with me directly about facilitating this study, please don't hesitate to contact me at louann.mokwa@gmail.com

Endnotes

Session 1

1   Charles R. Swindoll, *Esther, A Woman of Strength and Dignity* (Nashville: Thomas Nelson Publishers, 2006), p. X.

2   John F. Brug, *Ezra, Nehemiah, Esther,* of The People's Bible series (Milwaukee: Northwestern Publishing House, 1985), p. 65.

3   Brug, p. 165.

4   Beth Moore, *Esther: It's Tough Being a Woman* (Nashville: Lifeway Press, 2008), p. 7.

5   *Illustrated Dictionary of the Bible* (Nashville: Thomas Nelson Publishers, 1986), p. 123.

6   NIV Study Bible, notes.

7   NIV Study Bible, notes.

8   *Illustrated Dictionary of the Bible*, pp. 153,154,356,357.

9   Pastor Ben Kempfert, 2020.

10   Earl Radmacher, Ron Allen, and H. Wayne House, *Compact Bible Commentary* (Nashville: Thomas Nelson Publishers, 2004), p. 323.

11   Swindoll, p. 25.

12   Radmacher, Allen, and House, p. 323.

13   NIV Study Bible, notes.

14   *The New Complete Works of Josephus,* translated by William Whiston, commentary by Paul Maier (Grand Rapids: Kregel Publications, 1999), p. 374.

15   Brug, p. 162.

16   Brug, pp. 159,160.

Session 2

17 Brug, p. 165.

18 Brug, p. 166.

19 *The New Complete Works of Josephus*, p. 374.

20 NIV Study Bible, notes.

21 *The New Complete Works of Josephus*, p. 375.

22 Radmacher, Allen, and House, p. 325.

23 *Illustrated Dictionary of the Bible*, p. 359.

Session 3

24 *The New Complete Works of Josephus*, p. 375.

25 NIV Study Bible, notes.

26 *Life Application Study Bible* (Wheaton, IL: Tyndale House Publishers, 1966), p. 771.

27 Radmacher, Allen, and House, p. 325.

28 NIV Study Bible, notes.

29 Brug, p. 172.

30 *Illustrated Dictionary of the Bible*, p. 889.

31 Swindoll, p. 71.

32 *The New Complete Works of Josephus*, p. 375.

Session 4

33 Radmacher, Allen, and House, p. 325.

34 NIV Study Bible, notes.

35 *The New Complete Works of Josephus*, pp. 376,377.

36 Radmacher, Allen, and House, p. 326.

Session 5

37 *The New Complete Works of Josephus*, p. 377.

38 Brug, p. 180.

39 Brug, p. 180.

40 *The New Complete Works of Josephus*, p. 377.

41 Moore, p. 114.

42 NIV Study Bible, notes.

Session 6

43 Swindoll, p. 118.

44 *The New Complete Works of Josephus*, p. 378.

45 *The New Complete Works of Josephus*, p. 379.

Session 7

46 Brug, p. 190.

47 NIV Study Bible, notes.

48 Radmacher, Allen, and House, p. 328.

49 Radmacher, Allen, and House, p. 328.

50 Brug, p. 191.

51 Radmacher, Allen, and House, p. 329.

52 Brug, p. 193.

53 *Life Application Study Bible*, p. 779.

54 Brug, p. 196.

55 Brug, p. 197.

56 Swindoll, p. 189.

57 Radmacher, Allen, and House, p. 328.

58 Radmacher, Allen, and House, p. 329.

Answer Key

59 *Life Application Study Bible*, p. 766.

60 NIV Study Bible, notes.

61 Brug, p. 162.

62 Biblegateway.com, accessed 9/4/2020.

63 Brug, pp. 166,167.

64 NIV Study Bible, notes.

65 NIV Study Bible, notes.

66 *Illustrated Dictionary of the Bible*, p. 38.

67 Daniel J. Habben, "Our shelter in God's shadow," *Forward in Christ*, Vol. 106, No. 7, July 2019. Accessed from https://wels.net/our-shelter-in-gods-shadow/, accessed 6/29/21.

68 Ulpan.com, accessed 9/5/2020.

69 *Life Application Study Bible*, notes, p. 1310.

70 Brug, p. 176.

71 Radmacher, Allen, and House, p. 326.

72 Werner H. Franzmann, *Bible History Commentary: Old Testament* (Milwaukee: Northwestern Publishing House, 2000), pp. 388,389.

73 Franzmann, p. 430.

74 David G. Scharf, "Serving as God made me," *Forward in Christ*, Vol. 103, No. 6, June 2016. Accessed from https://wels.net/serving-as-god-made-me/, accessed 7/1/21.

75 Scharf.

76 NIV Study Bible, notes.

77 NIV Study Bible, notes.

Acknowledgments

About a year ago, God placed in my lap an opportunity to lead the Immanuel women's Bible study. With a prayerful heart, much hesitation, and encouragement from Pastor Ronald Siemers, I facilitated Naomi Schmidt's study of *Ruth: Living in God's Unfailing Faithfulness.* The steadfast sisters in the Bible study encouraged me further by their loyal attendance, and we moved on to Pastor Mark Paustian's *Prepared to Answer,* which sharpened our knowledge in some of the familiar stories and teachings of the Bible. Our goal was to better equip ourselves when answering and speaking the truth about God's Word, especially to nonbelievers.

Facilitating these studies required me to delve deeper than ever into the Bible. Guided daily by the Holy Spirit, I began to prepare a personal leader's guide to accompany Pastor Paustian's book. Every morning, while I prepared to write, doubt and fear would creep in; but after some time in prayer—once I opened the Bible—those feelings departed and the work continued.

When I was looking to our next study, the book of Esther was intriguing. There are a few women's studies on this book; but using the study skills I developed while preparing for the two previous studies, I leapt into the abyss to create my own study. What I have learned is that God's Word is infinite in its meaning and wisdom. Reading certain stories or passages one day can provide new insights and deeper understanding of God's saving plan for us. With that said, what I read, studied, and wrote is a snapshot of Esther during the time I wrote it. I am sharing it and encouraging each one of you to write down your own thoughts as you read. If you have questions, dig deeper; I promise you, God will not disappoint.

There are a few people who deserve my gratitude for completion of this project. At the top of this list is God, my Lord and Savior, who has given us eternal life through his Son, Jesus Christ, and the gift of his Holy Word. My husband, Jim, who has supported me in my "retirement," giving me the ability to pave this new path forward. My sisters in Christ who participate in the Immanuel women's Bible study, they have tolerated my novice leadership and have taught me so much. I thank you and praise God for each one of you. Pastor Ben Kempfert, who graciously agreed to be plagued with reviews of my draft. Thank you for your insights and sharing your amazing knowledge of God's Word. And lastly, my wordsmith and informal editor, Cheryl Diener, who has committed her life to praising our living Savior, Jesus Christ.

To God be the glory!

Lou Ann Mokwa